That Fall

New & Selected Poems

PAUL GENEGA

salmonpoetry

Published in 2001 by
Salmon Publishing Ltd,
Cliffs of Moher, Co. Clare, Ireland
http://www.salmonpoetry.com
email: info@salmonpoetry.com

Coyright © Paul Genega 2001
The moral right of the author has been asserted.

A catalogue record for this book is available from the British Library.

ISBN 1 903392 16 0 Paperback

All rights reserved. No part of this publication may be reproduced or transmitted in any form or by any means, electronic or mechanical, including photography, recording, or any information storage or retrieval system, without permission in writing from the publisher. The book is sold subject to the condition that it shall not, by way of trade or otherwise, be lent, resold or otherwise circulated without the publisher's prior consent in any form of binding or cover other than that in which it is published and without a similar condition, including this condition, being imposed on the subsequent purchaser.

Front Cover Image: *Thorn Tree, Clare*, by Margaret Irwin
Typeset by Siobhán Hutson
Printed by Offset Paperback Mfrs., Inc., PA

Acknowledgements

Grateful acknowledgment goes to the editors of the following publications in which some of these poems first appeared:

New York Quarterly, Akros Review, The Nation, Home Planet News, The Panhandler, Poetry Motel, Free Lunch, The Ohio Journal, The New Jersey Review of Literature, Poetry, Footworks, Three Mile Harbor, The Passaic County College Poetry Center Anthology, Yearbook of American Poetry, Outerbridge, Joe Soap's Canoe (England), Washington Review, Pudding, Webster Review, Southwest Review, Overtures, The Paterson Literary Review, The Literary Review, Tvodnik Powszechnv (Poland), Crosscurrents, Rhino, Greensboro Review, Epoch, and Apocalypse Now.

"Epic", "The Missing Year", "Istanbul", "Saint Elvis", "The Oyster" and "The Fairy Tale Fathers" also appeared in *Kings & Beggars* (San Francisco: GLB Publishers, 1993). "Aliens", "Postcards from Silence", "Descent and Sentiment", "The Rainmaker", "Memorial to Labor Day", "That Summer", "The Self-Made Man" and "The Courier" also appeared in *Striking Water* (Salmon Publishing, 1989).

Special thanks to Aaron Fink for his etchings based on the poems; Jeff MacMahon for including "The Courier" at Dance Theater Workshops; Barry Brian Werger for his robotic installation of "The Self-Made Man"; Patty Stotter for her musical setting of "Cassandra"; Ann Katcher for her unflagging support at Three Mile Harbor Press; Chris White for his jazz collaborations at Bloomfield College; Enid Dame and Don Lev for giving the poems Home; Toni Levi for the many years of detailed critique; Bloomfield College for a sabbatical to bring this book to completion; and Jim Werkowski for keeping the home fires burning.

Contents

I

The Abandoned Barn	3
Tide Line	6
Neon	7
The Fathers' Room	8
Fat Silence	9
Brooklyn	10
Roomer	12
What Then	13
Change of Seasons	15

II

In Dark Days	23
Neighbors	24
Dreams &	25
Mangrove	26
Sailing Away	28
Smoke	29
Awful Tender	30
W Street: 1969	31
Letter from the Cul-de-sac	32
She	34
The Work	35
As It Happens	37
Purple Buddha	39
The Day After	42

III

Reconsidering the Cat	45
Lavender Mist	46

Belle Rêve	47
Renfield's Song	48
Cassandra	49
Clytemnestra	50
Remains	51
The Monk	54
Parable	55
Paradiso Di Pinocchio	56
Ironclad Aardvark	57
Mugwumps, VA	58
The Undertoad	59
Marie's Barrette	61
Love Poem	62
The Secret Life	64
Are You a Painter?	65
I Lifted the Lid On the Black Enameled Box...	67

IV

Descent and Sentiment	73
Memorial to Labor Day	74
Aliens	76
The Missing Years	78
The Courier	80
Safe Places	83
The Rainmaker	84
The Fairy Tale Fathers	86
Epic	88
Istanbul	89
Postcards from Silence	90
Saint Elvis	92
The Oyster	93
The Self-Made Man	95

I

The Abandoned Barn
for Felice Nudelman

The abandoned barn stands in a field
of rudbeckia and loosestrife,
so close to the road
rust and splinters shower
whenever a car passes by.
Its public side, where a weary red hangs on,
is overgrown with sumac, moonvine and poison ivy.
A rotted path of two-by-fours
leads to the door; its padlock, fist-
sized, will not budge.

The north and east sides,
facing my yard,
have weathered winter grey
or a deeply burnished brown.
Almost small and self-effacing
from the road, the barn
looms large from my hillside,
a stolid ark sailing purple-yellow seas.

Pigeons inhabit the uppermost story.
The males do a dance on the window sill there,
strutting and bobbing, turning, whirling, weaving,
all puffery and low coo
for their coyly bored intended.
Comical, violent, stock, undebonair,
they look like a feathered Punch & Judy.

In late spring flickers join them,
drumming the tin roof,
luring love with percussive jazz.
Sometimes seeming spent, dispirited, confused,
they cling to the sides and peck listlessly
at wood knots, the picture of teenage despair.

And once one brazen bird
drilled a hole – from inside – and
white rump boldly flashing, flew quietly away.

Around the cracked foundation
the ground is wet and spongy.
Cattails rise in summer; mud sucks at shoes.
The lowest window, a jigsaw of black glass,
is still too high to reach
but there are gaps in the planks
and on a very bright day
if I wade through brush and bramble
and risk the poison ivy, I can see inside.

On the left, at the outer edge of vision,
is some sort of machine –
blades, cogs, pincers, teeth –
mysteriously lovely like all things utilitarian
once they have outlived their purpose.
On the right: three open grain casks,
burlap bags marked Rye Seed
and an ancient workhorse collar,
half the leather missing,
spewing entrails of straw.
Otherwise the barn is empty –
dim, dank, visceral and huge.

Some nights, especially in autumn,
if I've ignored the barn all day
or have been all day preoccupied with it,
I dream myself inside. Inside... the dream...
are fecund smells and silence
like an ocean underground.
And inside it is dark
and light at the same time,
not shadowy or dismal
but luminous and quickening,
the difference between silver and grey.

The machine against the wall
is the helm of a great schooner;
the casks and bags, gold cargo;
the collar, my first mate;
and with skull and cross bones flying,
I sail, I sail away

through lightning and loosestrife,
rudbeckia and whitecaps,
wind and water pouring through the walls,
rain battering the roof
like a thousand one flickers
or a Caribbean steel band;
we sail, we sail away,
both in the sea and of it,
landlocked and oceanic,
inside and yet outside,
myself and something different –

until the ripe smells alter
to aromas uncomfortably familiar
(like burnt toast)
and the sound becomes expectant
(like a man clearing his throat)
and the opalescent silver wanes into pastel,
until I've sailed back to my childhood
then I wake, slick with the salt of the dream.

A broken weather vane crowns a little cupola
on the barn at the edge of my world.
It reads:

<pre>
          I

     W   E

          S
</pre>

The arrow points always to I.

Tide Line
for Priscilla Orr

Walking the rip tide line,
wrackweed and whelk shells
crunching underfoot,
catamaran, stripped of sails
beating time with its halyard,
gulls winging their way
through deepening mauve,
tern plunging for a fish

I think myself Ulysses
back on the familiar beach
of his long island,
the pebble-strewn shore
before Sophocles or sophistry
where he first dared the breakers,
went after a flounder,
woolgathered about God

Ulysses, fresh off the boat,
greenhorn in his own land,
listening half-cocked
to the self-insistent crunch,
walking up courage for home,
some mist-enveloped small town
where the grocer's face is friendly
and the same old elms give shade

lost, of course, lost
in the wake of profit's progress,
raked like resort sand,
razed now like the waves
which sloshed the amber bottle
with the sour mash of myth –
August sun fast sinking
to its own gaudy applause

Neon

The heroic canvas
Las Vegas
The whole town hot
With it

Or Times Square
Where the bare glare
Is sexier
Than a wurlitzer

But it's the miniature
I most admire
Swain's red
On clapboard

Surrounded by pine
Where the same nine
Guys nurse beers
And Saturday lasts years

Wherever that glow
I know I must go
In, finally home
Bellied up and   *EL* *OME*

The Fathers' Room

At this window you can look into
the room in which the fathers gather.
It is hot in the room. The fathers sit in
undershirts, white straps stuck to shoulders.
All the fathers are drinking from cans,
taking long gulps, wiping the spillover
off their chins with knuckles.
There is an amber bottle on the table
but no ice. The room is filled with smoke
but not all the fathers smoke. Fathers
that do smoke, chain smoke from red packs.

The game they are playing is poker,
five card stud. The blue and red
chips on the table is the ante.
There is no telling if the fathers do much
bluffing. There is no telling
what father-talk they do
since the windows are kept closed.
But when the game is finished,
the fathers will towel-off, button shirts
and leave. If you want, then, you may
enter, and touch one of their towels.

Fat Silence

Like lard.
Like the bacon grease
We kept
Lest it clog the sink.

Cold lard.
White, smooth, hard.
Bits of bacon
Like shrapnel embedded.

Oiler than butter.
Bad for the heart
And arteries.
Touched,

It made us queasy –
Coating our thumbs
And only spread thinner
By tap water.

Thus we kept it
In the fridge.
Tin upon tin
Safely lidded.

How quickly it would
Puddle, if warmed –
Sizzle and spit
Put on the warring flame.

Brooklyn
for Steve Golin

The transistor radio
was black and compact,
about the size of my shoes.
Tucked under the pillow
while everyone else slept
it brought music which brought
Brooklyn into my split level life.

Shoop-shoop, doo-lang, schur-woop, shang-shang
and I'd slip to a place
built entirely of hormones
to slouch on dark street corners
with three guys all named Tony
and wait for what-
the-hell-may-come to come.

Some nights, especially in September,
back from a week in the Poconos
with family, the tedium begun,
momentous events might occur –
like a car chase after mobsters,
fist fight with black leather
or a cold, red can of beer –
but most nights we just talked loud,
said *fuck* as if we owned it
and waited for life to begin.

It always did –
three Bazooka-popping girls, all Sheilas,
hipswinging down the street,
crowns of lacquered blondness,
mascaraed eyes, white lipstick,
dresses slit up to their thighs.

Then winking sly winks,
slicking their hair back
with steel combs, just so,
grinning grins of uncrackable composure,
the Tonys would wolf-whistle
and the Sheilas fell instantly in love.

In that Brooklyn of my dreaming
Sheilas were always at-hand –
loudly clapping, cheering
when the Tonys formed The Heartaches
and sang "My Love Needs" at the Fox
or when there was a big dance
called A Enchanted Evening
and everyone was going with a date
or when Tonys felt the dark heat
burning their black pants
after a U-Bet eggcream

and instead of going home
to read *Silas Marner* or *O Pioneers!*
the Tonys and the Sheilas
sat down on a stoop
lamplighted soft yellow,
each Tony with a Sheila
(now pony-tailed, pearl perfect)
his bare arm draped around her,
face inching close, slow motion,
eyes shut, wet lips ready –

and I'd find that I was rising,
rising, rising, rising
to the top
of the Coney Island Parachute Jump ride
up I'd go, up, up,
all of misty, magic Brooklyn
stretching out before me
like a lawless Promised Land –
inchoate, hard-edged, silly, almost sweet,
and new as the new of that fall.

Roomer

He lived in the attic under the eaves.
Grandmother said he was a nice young man.
Whenever I visited, I'd sneak upstairs
To inspect the space he inhabited –
Iron bed covered with blue blankets,
Chifforobe with tweed jacket, straw
Valise which was always, always locked.
How stark and neat, I marveled,
The life of a nice young man was.

Then one day he was gone. And grandmother
Would say only he wasn't a nice young man
After all. Face flushed, I rushed
Upstairs to see – sure enough,
His things had vanished; the window
Had been opened; the iron bed, stripped –
Two old woolen blankets lying crumpled
On the floor, like the shed wings
Of an angel, like a sigh in bas-relief.

What Then

of that woman
in babushka, black wool
blooming roses,
blood-red near the fringe —

eyes like night sky
lying on flesh pillows —

blub-lipped,
Mongol cheekboned —

her body, all Ukraine —

that woman, dear old woman
farting cabbage soup
and creamed beets
in a thin dress
in a small house
in suburban New York sprawl —

who, wishboned with arthritis,
legs marbled like good steaks

squatted in manure
to set down lima seeds,

who proffered ripe tomato
as if summer itself

who plucked carrots
out of wet loam
and bid me eat them raw —

that woman, she alone
in a family subsisting
on crazy and self-hatred

who urged the boy-me read
books that she could not,

who loved my sprouting face hairs
because they looked like hers,

who pressed upon me
three times
folded fives "for fun" —

that woman
who in steerage
had fled mud-floor,
vodka father
and the start of the tsar's war

and who, had she remained
would have eagerly,
religiously,
unquestioningly,
excitedly

delivered her "Jew neighbors"
to Treblinka, Baba Yar —

what then of that woman,
and the guilt, the love, the knowing

what might have been,
what could have been,
what was, what was, what was

Change of Seasons

1. That Summer

That summer we stacked notions
on the cobweb shelves of Levin's Five & Dime.
Nights, returned from love in the last row
of the loge, we walked the pine grove
father had planted when he first married

our home. With each hard step we took
rustling the brush, a dove whooshed
from the treetops — the sky flushed
into frenzy until the dark wings beating
terrified us inside, naked on our beds.

All that summer the sky appeared
crooked, untrustworthy,
like a friend caught in a lie.
Once, as if a habit reprimanded daily
had been performed one too many times

the air assumed a mean-spirited silence
then loosed a paean of rage —
clouds dropping
to the townhall tower clock,
sending hands flying, battering its face...

Later, sky ascended to a high
whistle of blue, everywhere there were
butterflies, kissed to life
by some breathtaking enchantress,
borne by a wind we both wanted to own.

And that summer also grandmother lay dying
on a leased hospital bed. If nobody was
looking, we would crank her up to sitting
and proffer a craved cookie, delighting
as she snatched it like a shy, wild bird.

Already more avine than human that summer,
she sometimes attracted others
of her kind — starlings by the hundreds
descending on the driveway, the pinetum,
the garden, the lawn chairs, the door...

But the old woman did not fly
that summer while we stayed
vaguely ill — humorless
and dizzy, ravaged by itches
we could not seem to quell.

Flushed one night with fever,
stumbling past curfew, we first
discovered even home could change —
in mother's greenhouse a cereus had exploded,
its heavy mauve odor coating every room.

Drunk on a beer and the mere thought
of that flower, bent on reaching
an intoxicated pitch, we snuck
our first sweet brandies and waited
for sunrise to watch the flowers die.

They did not die, however, just as nothing
that summer worked the way we'd thought.
Wax lips, those blooms lasted for weeks,
their sex and death smell lingering
in the pines, in the loge, at Levin's,

in our beds — lingering like that summer
when anything could happen, that summer
when everything and nothing seems to happen,
that summer which lingers, lingers and lingers,
like the long adolescence of American men.

2. That Fall

Leaves came down in a quick brown tumble.
We raked in the rain,
scratching our way to the curb.
But the county collectors never came
that fall. The leaves blew back.
No gloved hands to haul them away,
the fire ban strictly enforced.

The dog danced on the oaken lawn,
the make-believe ballroom of our land.
One night we found a family of overweight doves,
their small faces staring at the moon
as if waiting for someone
to get up and change the channel.
Off they went in a yammer of petty irritation

and we saw ourselves at the supermarket,
post office, bank... all the long lines of our lives.
Sometimes that solid world sent emissaries.
A mailman in tan slicker slid letters
through the slot, some addressed
to Resident, some which knew our names.
We let them lie unopened, knee-deep on the rug,
a morass of manila disappointments.

In a fall that brown
we should have anticipated red –
the ambulance at the door flinging its lights,
your lungs collapsed to a lacquered family locket.
The dog watched as they hauled you away
then waltzed outside and died.
But you did not.

Back you were the next night
to shroud the dog in moon.
Doves keened like mail-order mourners.

Wind prayed as wind does.
And having thusly mustered what we could of worship,
the clocks set back and accurate,
we settled into silence – sipped,
sighed and watched the empire decline.

3. That Winter

In the winter of my childhood
I would lace dream skates
and glide the night on steel.

On the moon-lake it was cold,
so cold my screams were frozen
as the ice began to spider-web,
creak, moan, crack, give way...

And down I'd plunge to darkness,
colder and darker than anything
I'd known, crashing into water,
thrashing in that water, clawing,
scratching, searching for the hole,
for the place where I had entered –

until with crystal logic,
the kind which dreams supply,
I'd remember there was air
embedded in the ice and I'd
put my lips up to it and
gingerly, I'd breathe, swim
about some more and breathe,
swim about some more and breathe...

That little air pocket keeping me
alive in the cold, in the dark,
in the winter of my childhood
when even my dreams had me drowned.

4. That Spring
for Jim Werkowski

when the ice wept, that first spring
in the house, the earth gave bloom
to garbage — glass, steel, aluminum,
asbestos — decades of debris oozing up
from the mud. And there where we'd
envisioned foxglove and phlox,
asparagus and lilies, arose
an ancient boxspring, rusted, barbed
and ours, that spring, all ours.
Like the dogwoods and the shagbarks,
vines of poison ivy, the sulfurous
water of the well. So long city
renters, we claimed and named
all in our domain, sallying out
each morning as if we worked
for the greedy Queen of Spain.
And that boxspring too, that island
of iron, we claimed that spring,
we loved — every spike and coil,
every saber-like joint, every screw.
We placed it on the porch
with the twig chairs and the rag rugs,
a kind of Adirondack/Inquisition decor.

And there it stayed that spring
while we converted from our city ways,
adjusted to life without sirens
or lox. Until one day in May,
around the time the biting flies emerged,
I caught my heal on the corner and...
such blood! You sprang to get a band aid
but before you got back the jaw
already locked. Not tetanus. Fear,
just a case of catholic fear. Too happy,
I thought, within these mortal coils,

too much in blooming love
for a fading middle age,
I read the blood reminding us
of what must someday come.
"Hold me!" I cried when the pain
reformed as language. "The English
queen is jealous. The pirate
wants our gold." You held on
and we fell on the spring
that spring together, dukes of debris,
stewards of the landfill with a faint
jesuitical whiff of down below.

II

In Dark Days

In dark days, in days of rain and mud
I have gone looking for my village
ribbed prairies I have crossed
clouded mountains I have climbed
looking for my village
around tables of talk, passionate, polite
among those who write poetry
who hate greed
who wait to watch the hawk soar
who make love in the manner I make love

I have gone looking for my village
in the dusty halls of educators
in the palaces of curios
in the neon buzz of now
in malodorous smoke
in paranoid powder
in amber tumbler glass
in theater, in politics
in the gloaming, by the sea
back in the housing tract where I was a boy
and all the places since my life has been my own
I have sought, I am seeking

Neighbors

Apartment 6C is available, the old woman
across the hall informs me. He seemed
so sweet, she says. Yes, I say, yes,
he seemed a nice young man. I live
in 7C. Our walls almost touched.
Sound crossed the wood and plaster easily.
Sometimes he played rock and my space
shook to his mood. And sometimes, late,
there were faint strains of Satie and we
were sad together. My apartment forms
an "L." From my kitchen window I could
look into his bedroom. Once he was in bed.
On his bare chest, a green book. All night
I dreamed in green. We'd say hello
on the elevator, talked weather on the way
down. Winters he wore a camelhair coat
and looked like a kid playing dressup.
His hair was sandy; his eyes sea grey.
The last time I saw him, his eyes had
sunk deep into his skull, tide pools
from a storm cast high onto pale rock,
evaporating, unreplenished. He'd lost
half himself already. So fragile, thin.
It was cold. And now the old woman
across the hall informs me Apartment 6C
is available. I sit in my life and stare past
the dirty window. The room I see is dark,
the city less than a decibel quieter.

Dreams &

dreams ago
the ice settled in

winters following winters
prairies opening in snow

winds of fierce and purposeful howl
baring their white teeth

whip, lance, stiletto, razor blade

The small house in bondage
stoic through the onslaught

tea in blue chipped cups
fire fading in the grate

road which leads to roads
buried and buried

for good

Mangrove

Green lies like a bandage on the bay.
Dusk, we cool ourselves on the dock.
You drink vodka. I have a coke
with a cherry. I love the white hiss
when the sodapop is poured, the dark
ball at the bottom. And I love
the dark brown pelicans that fly by,
leather birds from the Dinosaur Age.
Back then, our part of Florida
did not attract tourists, just those
highwaisted, hipflasked fishers
from up north. Swigging, they start
staring. It's as if I am trapped
in some filthy, cracking mirror
smeared thick with bad years.
My legs want to run, but I wind up
standing, staring. I more than earn
their dimes. Your smiling seemed
similar. I remember the old outboard –
the moan, the belch, the smell
of dying factory, smoke lobbing along
the shore. You and me and whatever
highwaisted fisherman was around
would take the old skiff bayside
angling for grouper or trout.
More than sleep, I hate that part –
curling through the mangrove,
its thicket of gnarled branches,
the impenetrable interior where
anything might live – a jawed and
scaly thing waiting a millennium
for one human mistake. Each tug
on the line is a terror, convinced
we've snagged the waiting one.
But we only catch branches, sometimes

sad fish, while you and the stranger
drink into a slur. By then the sky
had gobbled the last wormy pink
so we head back to the dock.
Quickly, I leap up, wrap a wet line
around a pylon, secure the boat
just right. Now my fear can settle down
as the bay settles down and the night
comes on a steady pulse of crickets
and stars. Safe, I thought, we're safe.
But out there, I knew, it too was
settling down, sinking into mud.
It had all the time in the world.
Like the slow rowing pelicans and
the preacher's Sweet Jesus and like
me back then, poised on the edge
of a world not land or water —
you and me and the stranger in
the mangrove, those first few years
after they took mama away.

Sailing Away

Water was wool, tightly woven
but thin piled, scratch-bristly, drab gray.
Flat on my belly, arms flailing
like hooked fish, I drank dust and I swam.
Danger flashed fins, unfurled sticky tentacles,
rushed through the flood gates I opened.
In the shallows, in the shadows,
I found glittering white pebbles
snatched from a neighbor's yew garden –
soft green, new green, yellow-green –
out there, in a world of sunshine and air,
a world of sunshine where boys were
lost and everything, she said,
where boys were lost to everything.

So I sailed, I sailed away,
there in the small box of the room.
I sailed, I sailed away.
Until he came home and beat me
for not playing boy-games outdoors.

Sail, sailing away...
And when I came at last to Ulysses
and we wedged the stalwart ship
into roiling straits,
faced the deadly suck of whirlpool,
the giant's hungry jaws,
I knew their names, I knew them,
and why the darkest lotus leaves taste good.

Smoke

Smoke curling
from a cigarette,
slow in a windowless
room, is made of
words unspoken,
whole sentences
repetitive like
dreams born on
the tip of fire
and gone; we try
to read what we
needed – will
need – need –
one after another
building up like
history, a love-
less time we try
to grind out
only to relight

Awful Tender
for Ann Katcher

The dog is dying in the middle of the road

he lies on his side
soft mass of hard breathing
brown eyes like huge pennies
melted into sockets
struck with the knowledge

he is dying in the middle of the road

head turned from the flanks
of well-tanned beach-tog teens
each smudged with a guilty
this ain't my fault, man look
wanting to be seated
routinely at the table
not *for Chrissakes* standing

in the middle of a road, watching a dog dying

old woman crouched beside him
whispering and stroking
whispering, soft stroking
looking up, unblinking
as a dark car slows, then passes

to the middle of the night

where the dog goes on with dying
and her soft hand goes on stroking
no volley of fine platitudes
to finish them both off
or loose the awful
tender of that scene

W Street: 1969

Young we were then — very. Children
playing house in sundry peeling apartments,
concocting awful eggplant casseroles,
winning non-virginity with all
the awkward tenderness we owned.

Talking then and talking
around a three-legged kitchen table,
talking of it, talking, the one talk
talked unceasing — out there — through
that window — out there — was a war.

The long lupine hours, new to us,
all spoke of it. And the yammering birds
of the sunrise. And the pipes which groaned.
The floorboard creaks. And one day
Diane or Caroline or Linda
threw another awful casserole
on the stained formica table and

she screamed. That scream, it said that someone,
a someone I knew though now the name is lost,
had cut his finger off
because his CO had been denied,
had cut his finger off because
his CO had been denied, had cut
his finger off because he'd been
denied... had cut off... been denied...

Lost we were then — very. Children
peeling tenderness in sundry eggplant houses,
concocting awkward window casseroles,
warring our virginity with all
the winning awful

It...
still pointing

Letter from the Cul-de-Sac

    On this block houses
    line up, rigid as soldiers —
    backs straight, chests puffed out,
    wary eyes fixed east, as if
    guarding the darkness inside

"All these Long Island towns seem somehow old now,
not the makeshift suburbs we knew as kids.
The sycamores full shade trees. Hedges high around each plot.
Often I feel lost here, not quite of this century —
nursemaid to that woman best with strange infections
unarrestable, companion to poor father,
so powerfully unhappy since arthritis killed his practice.

Sundown, she's asleep, so nights it's just the two of us
slouching into silence around the big blonde table
till father fetches wine. Wine these days, you see,
is father's pride and joy. He studies wines, collects,
catalogues, critiques, had a cellar put in recently
climate-controlled, padlocked, to store those he loves best.

Great wine, I've come to realize, truly is a miracle —
the weather, the soil, all must be just perfect.
Heavy rains cause root rot. Meager rain, dwarfed crops.
Then the vintner's care fermenting, casking, the wait...

Last night's, *mon cher, un vin extraordinaire,*
A *Côte de Nuits*, full-bodied, virile, midnight red.
O I know you would have liked it. Though for us
le vin est different; for us, it's an event —

    father eases the cork stopper like gloved hands
    raising a flag, slowly, so so slowly, till we hear
    the bottle kiss. Then he colors the *ballon,*
    swishes, sniffs, sips — *yes* means we can drink.

Some nights his yes proves maderized, overripe
or cloying. But most nights it is heaven –
yes yes yes in quick succession and waves of wine
keep falling, a red tide lovely, fragrant, unarrestable...

      it's as if we two were stranded
      on whispering-close islands
      bridged only by green glass...

But of course I think of you then and those
clanky iron bridges from your island of concrete,
how I hope you'll pay a visit once
mother shows improvement and provided it's not raining
for poor father's hands shake and fist
when it is raining, like now, *yes* it is raining
without sign – *yes*– it will clear."

She

In brackish weed of lake
bloom and autumn hum
she comes whitening the silt.
Slip sheer and dainty toe,
here and then, misplaced,
her breath a gallows wind,
quick shimmer of a sumac,
red, red, red and gone.
Love and life lost,
life and love lamented,
she wanders in the wilt.
Hound sad and papery,
skin like river rock,
a dimple in the logic
of the land. Wistful shade,
lingering like slow bees,
wanting us to stay, then
and here, when the wood
is wide as four o'clock,
the language old
as a sapling snapped.

The Work

The Milmore Memorial,
Angel of Death and the Sculptor
Daniel Chester French

for Jerry Adelmann

How large the wings of Death are,
how heavy they look
drooping from her back.

Still, she must move swiftly
with her baggage. Here
she has startled a young sculptor
mid-stroke in his work.

This man clearly is not her choice
of subject. Under her cowl
both eyes are averted.

Her right hand holds white lilies
clutched like grim apologies,
exigencies, excuses –

as if to disavow
what the left is doing,
slipping around the chisel,
nudging him with chill.

The man's stare is unflinching,
uninterrupted by terror or rage.

Muscles flexed, keenly concentrating,
he seems almost pleased
to find her standing here –

comparing her mouth
to the sphinx lips he's been carving,
the angles of both noses,
bone lines of their cheeks –

measuring, coolly,
even at the very end,
his work against her profile.

As It Happens
for Bob Fuchs

1.
The blueberry explodes in my mouth —
sweet juice and pulp.
A bit catches in my cavities

and my tongue worries it.
For hours I am eating that berry.
So little, so long.

2.
I am not eating. All day
I think of the food I am not eating —

slick fat burgers, *schlag* on tartes, goose, cereal,
gumbos, jumbalaya, *sorbet*, squab, granola,
sizzling soup, oxtails, chanterelles, polenta —

all of this and more I am not eating.

3.
In the cold, thin air
sad bird sings so sweetly.

Sky: wondrous blue, enormous
and one small bird
there singing, mostly bones.

4.
The smaller I become
the larger the world is.

Each day my shadow shortens.
I don't take up much space.

5.
In the dark
he downs dreams
thick and salty.

6.
One I heard a bird sing.
Once my mouth had berry.

7.
Put me in the blue bag
my mother made for sleeping.

Line it O Lord
with chignonned feathers.

Purple Buddha

"This was one of Gil's Bottles," Rob says,
pouring out the wine. "It's an '83 Bordeaux.
Grand Crus. Bet it's expensive as hell."

"Thanks," I say, reaching for the glass.
"Thanks," I muster, thinking,
you shouldn't be drinking, Rob.
All the doctors say that. What sense
does it make to drink ginseng all day
then drink red wine all night?

"There must be twenty bottles just like it.
Maybe more. Amazing how much
he had crammed into that studio.
How many days till we hauled it all away?"

"Six," I answer, pausing.
"Sunday noon to Friday night."
Six full days, I recall, combing through
a lifetime, packing videotapes,
film scripts, sweaters, records, flatware,
paperbacks, photographs, jewelry, socks...

"Remember the pennies?" Rob asks,
almost grinning. "Remember all those pennies?"

"Oh yeah," I say, "there were lots."
Lots, yes, lots indeed, as many dull pennies as tears.

"Three hundred thirty-six dollars
in pennies alone," Rob announces, big grinning.
"I bought myself that winter coat with half."

"Nice," I say, glancing at the camelhair
flung on the end of the couch.
"Nice," I tell him, thinking,
wear it in secondhand health, my good friend.

Rob leans back, closes swollen eyes,
sputters, allows the silence to be.

"Did I tell you what I found in his letters?" he asks.

Yes, you did, I think.
"What?" I say, nearly whispering.

"Did I tell you?" he repeats, this time loud.

"No," I say, bracing for what's coming.

"Love letters!" he blurts, eyes opening,
as if this weren't the eighty-first time I had heard it,
as if he can't contain it anymore.
"Love letters from two summers ago
when I was working Scranton.
I was playing Mahler
and he was flying off to England,
all the way to God damn England,
to screw some fat ass Belgian priest."

"Oh," I manage, shaking. "Are you sure?"
Thinking please, *Rob, let it go. It's done now. Let it go.*

"Damn right I'm fucking sure.
I've got all of them right here...
Want to see?" he shouts,
waving a wad of white paper.

"No, not now," I say,
thinking *no, not now, not ever.*

40

"He made xeroxes of his own love letters.
Can you believe that? Duplicates
of his flowery piss prose.
And worse he didn't destroy them.
Even though he knew, must have known,
I'd find them. Why would he do that?
Can you explain that to me?"

Because he loved you, I think.
"No, I can't," I lie.

"That big fat purple Buddha.
Remember at the end with the lesions,
like a big fat purple Buddha?"

"Yes," I say remembering...
how I dream it every night,
the wracked distended body,
the purple mask, the death cough.
I dream it every night
and wake up sweating.

"I don't look that bad?" Rob asks,
rubbing the splotches on his arm.

"No," I reply, "no, of course not."
No, much more like a cat,
a purple spotted leopard
set anytime to strike.

"Good," he grunts, grabbing the glass, pouring.

L'chaim.

The Day After

I drove lead-eyed
to the beach
and parked in the lot
at Louse Point.

The sun rose
with the mean face
of a drunk, burning
with inchoate rage.

Thick fog, sticky
as June woolens,
unraveled in thin
skeins of mist

until I could see
water – the swift
tidal river wriggling
like silverfish into harbor,

the aqua of the shallows,
the dark slate
where the floor dropped,
the electric green/pink

of the slicks.
In the car sealed
like your coffin I sat
watching the ongoing water.

The moon and your smell were disappearing.
The moon and your face were
disappearing. The moon has your face
now disappearing.

III

Reconsidering The Cat

for Helen Adam

And once again the cat
was deemed abomination —
electric skin and glaring eye,
gravity and waggery, sprangle
upon waggle, roll upon prank.

Swept from stoops,
cats padded in the streets.
By torchlight people gathered
bearing pitchfork, net and adz.
And fast as cats they killed
the cats to rid village
earth of all abomination.

But there was no release
from fear. Folded
tight on blackest nights
they heard hisses in the oak tops,
saw a white claw cutting through.
Cat always up there watching,
biding its time, stretching,
arching among stars, set anytime

to pounce, to pummel, to strike —
bird, boll, spinning mouse, orb,
unraveling ball of dark yarns.

Lavender Mist
after Pollock

The eye rides the sunset,
quick and hungry as a tern,
plunges the deep wink
of the harbor –

swan skeins spreading tendrils
loop a winter white
of plum, circling dun
clam shells, whispered
into color by waves,

waves raising their heads
like any small salt animal,
teeth gleaming momentary
smiles, so many simple secrets
unresolved,

dissolved
like an oil slick on sugar,
like the slow fade
of old movies –

the labored propulsion
of the cormorants,
high sweep of grey gulls,
all manner of memory
in the bay sky, on the sand –

heavy mauve curtain
corded back for night –
troupe of ancient actors
anxiously waiting in the wings.

Belle Rêve

Silk tatters this evening I am

Humdrum moon insinuating self in slim glasses,
Each an hour, sipping, sipped away

Memory misted, edges re-refined

Swill spills (Blanche sloppy) so I swab
But mostly it-I-we go down down easy

Too many watermarks on cherry wood to care

Wish times I still did, wish too good sleep cured

Not cured though, more pickled,
Puckered sallow baby floating in a jar
Like you'd find in some sick circus

Torn tent, ulcerated animals, loud sour calliope,
A sneery night out for the crowd

I have
No
Crowd

Sun, moon, new air after rain, and you
Star, *The Evening Star*, now calling

Hard, bright, necessary, sad

Love, when you call, why is it always collect?

Renfield's Song
after Ginsberg

Master, there is a fly inside my cell
Master, the fly is buzzing, around the little room, the fly buzzing
Master, out there is dog and rat and partridge
Master, in here, only fly
Master, here no shadows except when I sleep
Master, six days I am gone sleepless
Master of the shadows, six days without sleep
Master, look upon and pity me, small as pauper's trash
Master, ideas escape when I am listening
Master, there are facts that I do not wish to know
Master, I know nothing
Master, I am too
Master, I want, I want most to be instinct
Master, I am want most
Master, my hands are scratchy little sparrows
Master, wolfing arms
Master, hawking legs
Master, O my mouth
Master, the moon has been ladled in my eyeballs
Master, white moon has been poured into my eye
Master, as I speak, they are boiling tripe somewhere
Master, as I speak, someone touches a soft heart
Master, how I swim seas of fingernail and wax hair
Master, what I swim and am the keen waves' yawn
Master, there are depths I only feel outside me
Master, there are deeps without a singing shore
Master, the fly buzzing
Master, fly was buzzing
Master, Master, fly
Master, fly
I am
Now fly

Cassandra

for Patty Stotter

"Listen quick while the words
are still my making. Inside others
are waiting, night-feathered and
clawed. Words, words, they fly
from poor Cassandra. Cassandra, poor
Cassandra, less a woman now than wind.

No one dares kiss these lips
which can't stop moving, dares touch.
See, real hands. Me, I see too
clearly. Even lids shut,
such dazzle, such sharp light.
Yes, pity her... us... me...

Like the moon, the living moon
which can tongue its way through
forest, nothing stops her. She is
his. I am she. I am Cassandra,
a flame which should be frozen,
a buoy in heaving seas lamenting

its own clapper. I toll. I toll
like fate. *She names the days. She*
am Cassandra, with the truth
which makes men shudder, which makes
them laugh. They'll soon be ash. All
but you, if you will listen while

she thinks this is her making.
Words, I give her words, unstoppable
as ocean, to roil around that once-proud
mouth. Drink, if you dare, but beware
I am Cassandra. *Mine.* I am the god's,
cursed with words skinned from the stars

Clytemnestra

Face abraded by water and sand,
she wears the mask of everyday death.

She might have sold you the last gold roll
of Christmas wrap, fly paper or 8c stamps.

She lives six blocks over in the part
of town you never thought your neighborhood.

She is the woman just ahead on the midnight
shopping line, clutching frozen peas and Tide.

You hold cream for morning coffee.
a bag of frozen bagels,

when your eyes meet,
something... strange.

Beyond the world's weather is the woman
who moves in the depths of will be-was,

where all is connected
and nothing is distinct

and comes at the whim of dark waves.
Which do not care.

No wonder her feet stumble
in the solids of the markets.

No wonder she topples glasses,
elbows you, tromps feet.

No wonder her children
have locked themselves inside

the attic cedar closet
where, dreaming of each other,

they lie like a litter of strays.

Remains
for Beth Joselow

1.
The day he strode into town
the lines of our palms
all began to move.
Broad streaks split into deltas
then withered. Angles closed up.
Some furrows deepened
and the older folk showed bone.
Our hands began to throb
the way arthritic hands throb
when the weather starts to change.

2.
Before the giant killer came
none of us had noticed
we were living in a shadow.
"But friends," the stranger said,
"How else can you explain
your mushroom complexions,
the propensity to rickets,
that your oak trees are dwarfed?"
Sister Lisa laughed. Her love
line snaked a sidewinder's path.

3.
Sister Lisa was charged
with a balanced committee
to investigate bonsai and moss.
Her report demanded action:
"Today the moon passed into June
and life and love crossed over.
We must brace ourselves for more."

Everyone clapped although
clapping was quite painful.
For the wounded, sutures
were freely applied.

4.
"Time to kill," the giant
killer said, so we led him to
our arsenal of armor and shields.
He left, still unprotected,
toting nothing but a slingshot
and Lisa's crystal ball.
That night the women drew
hot water while men soaped
their hands. There were very few
children, but those that
we had were scrubbed clean.

5.
Mother Lisa tells this legend:
"There was a time when we stood
tall as trees and the ground
was soft. green moss.
At night we buried our heads
in the fur of friendly dogs.
Fingers made music and all stood
in reach. We knew who we were
by looking at our hands
and observing what they did.
The lines were bold and clear then."

6.
The stranger lives in town now.
We live in a profusion of hot white
light. Everything has grown
but some things lack proportion.

Our hands often itch, frequently
are sticky. We sweat a great deal.
And though we commemorate
each evening by working up
a lather, always we find dirt,
remains beneath our nails.

The Monk
for Richard Hart

In a stone tower above cold sea
A monk dips a pinfeather
In boar blood, slowly, painstakingly
Copies swirls and lines, the lovely meander
Of the alphabet. All day on parchment
He duplicates the marks – some
Like waves, one a little tent,
This one a doorway and transom...
Fluke hook, viper, glacier cap, wave,
Dueling swords, scimitar, sun...
In this way he readies for the grave
Believing he is serving the Son
Of Man preserving the wholly holy words
Of a crumbled yellow scroll.
For this a thousand birds
Will give their feathers, for his bowl
Of blood a hundred boar will die –
To keep for all time the draft of a deed
To a sulfur spring near Delphi
Which the monk, a modern man, cannot read.

Parable

4 What man of you, having an hundred sheep, if he lose one of them, doth not leave the ninety and nine in the wilderness, and go after that which is lost, until he find it

among sweetfern, the shag of its back flecked with phlox and clover, up upon its hindlegs, dancing with a cloud?

5 And when he hath found it, he layeth it on his shoulders, rejoicing,

sweating, stumbling, groaning, cursing the hot chase, the crazed bleats which breaketh the blue quiet, cudgel kicks to ribcage, lance-sharp teeth.

6 And when he cometh home, he calleth together his friends and neighbours, saying unto them, Rejoice with me; for I have found my sheep which was lost.

And prepareth at once a feast for celebration; and bindeth together the legs of the lost sheep; and buildeth a fine fire; and taketh a blade for slicing the fat belly; and cooketh it with thyme and sage and mountain mint sprigs, picked in the far where the wild sheep dared roam.

Paradiso Di Pinocchio

begins with scissors
flying oil blue sky.

Steel glints in sharp light,
stretches, stretches

nearly to straight line,
bites down hard on the strings.

The wood he was
and the would-bes
turn blood-bone –

to touch
and to be
touched,

lionized, loved –

he feels the infinite
possibility of limbs.

Wind-warmed by ocean
the boy-man
holds a fish comb,
skips a nonpareil stone.

Even the farthest horizon
is here, now.

Shadows stay put,
nothing grows or slackens

and porpoises
leap
at his lies.

Ironclad Aardvark

Ironclad aardvark mistakes himself
for another armadillo, shambles
in the shadows of new dust.

The red-ribboned door
he thinks of as overt-
ure, failed backer's audition,
graduating 12th in your class.

Midges menace him.
Mockingbirds mock.

And here's the real turtle
with a word or two about his race.

Ironclad aardvark bestows
every scene with crypto,
snivels in the yanked pods
of unnamed conifers.

Under the djinn eye of the moon
he rolls up in himself tight,
sleeps fast, dreams in hot pursuit.

Mugwumps, VA

Who could fail to admire the mugwumps of VA,
sobriquets of pandemonium, little rascals?

Under eaves in Eames chairs, fish-bone thin,
all Lionels, mugwumps do what a mugwump's gotta do.

And O they do it well! All day they do it well.
Not a slouch in the lot, these perfect postures,

heedless of the need for steel wool or trout fly.
Neither young nor old nor in any way illicit,

the mugwumps, even inert, approach villanelle,
swinging back, swinging forth, swinging south

and east O North, a kernel of confusion
to us, mere *citoyens*, stuck with demo

derbies, -cracy, while you await
dead angels to peel your hand grenades.

The Undertoad
a song with shellfish
for Marty Kellman

Beware the terrible Undertoad –
He thirsts for the salty,
He hungers for bone.
On a throne
Wrapped in wrackweed
Some five fathoms down,
Stingray for scepter
And lobster for crown,
He is lord of the elvers,
The master of squid,
Prince of pearl oysters,
The high king of krill.
To his will
Bow the blowfish
Which puff with each whim
And the acolyte crabs
That clap pincers for him
Whenever he rises
On stringy slick knees,
Flicks his white thrash-cord
And whips the prone sea
To roll all her shoulders
And lunge for the shore,
With each lash dash faster,
Crash, sputter, spray, roar...
O the Undertoad's lasso,
A noose for your feet,
Can snag you and drag you
Just strokes from the beach.
Beware or he'll haul you
Out, out and below,
Beyond the waves breaking,
Beneath clouds of roe

Where fluke bang
Their clam drums
And halibut hum
A slow solemn nocturne
For swimmers who come
To the weedy dark kingdom
Some five fathoms deep,
Thirsting for salt
In a wild wet sleep.

Marie's Barrette

What lips, what nose,
what hair did Marie sport.

Shreds of
kelp cling
to hollow
barnacles,
pool polluted
with oil slick,
bass viscera.

But then did the barrette transform
her drear transom. Rhinestone extravaganza,
ice chips on the fuchsia,
sparkle in the sphinx eye
as he got a load of those pyramids.

(O politicized hormones,
for once please get it straight:
covet not the ultimate barrette)

Marie, Marie Mastrangelo,
I confess I loved you well,
better, baby, than a cosine,
better yet than rhomboid Rose.

Here, blown dry and older,
I try hard to be me
and hope you happy
somewhere, somewhere
far beyond this sea.

Love Poem

A poem about love, it was going to be
a poem about someone I'd loved.
I tried it first on pure bond paper,
a field of hopeful snow,
but the words were drunken soldiers
weaving their way home, tipping tipsily in twos,
singing *leider* off-key, loud.

So okay, I thought, let'em sleep it off.
Next day I determined discipline was needed –
rigor, regimen, tough-mindedness, form.
I bought a ream of blue-lined paper, extra fine point pen.
But all the men had hangovers,
fumbled grumpily from their bunks,
muttering Greek curses underneath rank breaths.

Atten-shun! I ordered them in line.
And all that day I drilled them
back and forth across the page –

I loved you You Iloved Loved Iyou Have I loved I have Loved Love loved love –

the entire regiment was snoring before taps.

Time to get tough, zap a little life into the bums.
But when I switched on Windows
blazoned on the screen
was the order for court martial.
I protested, implored, plea bargained, pitched a fit...

Dawn the next day,
my poem about love,
about someone I had loved,
was taken out and shot.

How sad the words looked blindfolded,
slovenly and grizzled, clutching their fistfuls of mums.
And the worst by far, if the worst can be imagined —

no one paused a single moment
to ask if I'd anything to say.

The Secret Life

In my secret self I really am a fireman.
My feet follow sirens instinctively,
dance to the rhythm of flames.
But I do not like smoke. Smoke makes me cough.
When they build a fire without smoke
I'll become one.

In my secret self I'm attorney for the defense.
I could knot the tongues of liars,
cajole a hanging judge. But
I hate to raise a ruckus. Honestly, I'm shy.
When they allow for no-fault murder
I'll become one.

In my secret self I'm a Comanche chief.
I look good in feathers, manly in a loincloth.
I whoop well and can handle a bow.
But I don't want to play the fallguy all the time.
When they discover a West without cowboys
I'll become one.

In my secret self I really am a surgeon.
I love sharp shiny knives, thin precision lines.
And interiors are interesting.
But I do not like blood. Blood causes me to faint.
When they invent a man without blood
I'll become one.

Are You A Painter?

When stowing raft always connect steel line to vessel
(by shackling painter to cradle using Eliot weak link).
  – Instructions for safety rafts, Orient-New London Ferry

for Aaron Fink

Sun up, wind down, sea smooth
as a baby's dimpled rear.
Crisis over, apocalypse averted.
Quick, stow the rafts, find a painter.

Are you a painter? No?
Then explain how that puce shirt
matches your torn socks,
that smudge of burnt umber on the chin.
You call that chopped liver?
Well, not like my grandma made.
Where's the onion, where's the egg?
Oh yes, you're a painter.
See how unconcerned you are
with the mundane and comestible.
You're a painter or you've imagined yourself one.
There's a garret in that brain of yours
somewhere, goatee, black beret.
And you have evident inclinations –
spiritual largess, sensitivity, nobility,
a Gericault look in your eyes.

We knew you'd see it our way.
Good, put on these shackles.
Left ankle, right. Now the arm holds.
For Chrissakes, please stop squirming.
These are the finest irons on the market.
Same chains Rothko wore, Pollock, Ernst –
chelated double-links. brass locks, weld-on keys
(in case you're a hot closet Houdini).

We have the cradle to screw you to right here.
Of course it isn't yours.
This was an emergency, a sudden squall, the fix.
You think we had time
to get the real beddy-bye
you rocked and reeled and mewled in?
Besides, the old thing is probably long gone —
yard sales, tag sales, garage sales, classifieds.
It's an unsentimental age we live in,
an anti-art art loving age.

But this cradle will do. See how strong it is.
Those are hardwoods, pegged, not nailed.
We'll stow it from that scaffolding
just above those abstract watercolor waves.
And if the sheets slip, if the raft drops,
if art's accident prevails...

Well, down you'll go, dear painter,
as in old airs, down down down
till the human voices wake us
and you'll drown.

I Lifted the Lid On the Black Enameled Box...

and that was the day,
July 3rd of '54,
when the sea was born,
not blue. I remember best
the way the sand
was sweating, dunes
of grasses swaying,
how the moon had
somehow dreamed herself
into the noon sky.
I remember red umbrellas,
wicker baskets, blankets,
a playground with a gate,

but wait, is someone
listening? It's true,
someone is listening.
Hello. How do you do?
I love you. Don't go.
Wait. Picture, try to
picture, what it's like
to be pure sound –
sets of jagged screeches,
undulating moans, the low
rolls which are lullabies,
and all of it pointless
without receiving ears.

Oh yes, my friend,
I know, it's a simple
schoolboy paradox,
but the simple truth
is painful – I am
nothing without you.

You understand yes friend?
You understand. O yes,
you with those ample,
beautiful detached lobes.
How well you do your
listening. Keep listening.
I will tell. I will tell.
What should I tell?

So much, to be honest,
seems less than really
vital now that I have
been reducted to a voice
inside a box. Reducted?
Reduced? The right word
is in here somewhere.
Purified? Strained?
Rarefied? Perfected?
Perfected, that seems
best. Sound, after all,
doesn't sweat or hunger —
except to be heard, and
like all things, to be
loved. Oh not for itself,
for sonorities or colors,
the soothing movement
of regular rhythms,
but for what it says.
And what I say,
friend, is this —

please, please, please
don't ever leave me.
Take this box home,
place it squarely
on your nightstand.
I will sing for you,
spin stories, whisper

death-bed truths
which matter, but
please, please, please
don't ever leave me.
If you want me to,
I'll flatter. I've lived
also behind mirrors.
I can chart the farflung
stars which excuse away
your failures, but please
don't, like my father,
like my mother, like the sea,
like the moon and red
umbrellas and my lovers
and the air, please,
please, please don't

    ...AND I SHUT IT.

IV

Descent and Sentiment

The plane makes its descent on
the city where I lived once, flickering
Interstates, cloverleaves and loops,
as if Omaha, exploded, had strewn
its ruby innards from sea to shining sea.
Still, there is the roc egg of the Capitol,
floodlit – there, Washington's white cock,
things recognizable amid the squat
flat-top office buildings, all built
since I've been gone. I remember D.C.

Southern – waxy magnolias, ornate columned
mansions of mustachioed ambassadors,
unbreathable summers, and you, dreamer,
drifter, odd-jobber, first honest love
in a rowhouse long ago. I remember that
whole summer beneath your sloping roof,
laughing at nothing, drinking too much
wine. We spoke three words through August
then firmly shook good-bye. Me, back
to Nebraska; you to Virginia, I think.

Now, here, buckled to my speeding seat,
I search, despite myself, for our
rowhouse gable, for the window strobed
with candles and moon, though surely razed.
Of course I cannot find it, more than count
these lights, the beds I've known since you.
By landing the runway is just a blur
of blue. Then the wheels touch, touch down
firmly, and the dim dishonest longing
for the long gone bursts in flame.

Memorial to Labor Day

I remember best the hours
after supper, watching the sea
violet, the thin summer sunlight
deepen, disappear. I remember the rhythm
of the porch swing which held father,
the roiling chowder pot that mother

scoured and re-scoured. Poor mother,
she seemed to spend all her hours
in the kitchen that summer. Neither father's
reprimands nor the cajoling of the sea
could dissuade her fierce rhythm
of more work and more. Daylight

gone, she retired. First light
of morning, back poor mother
was, battling the rhythm
of summer with her broom. One hour
alone she allowed herself sea-
side, muddling the tide pools. Father,

in all fairness, father
would beg her, relax, lighten
up, please, we're on vacation. But mother
couldn't care less. One hour with the sea
was enough, she'd snap back. And the hours
cooking, cleaning... Well, the rhythm

of life doesn't stop in Amagansett; the rhythm
of work never stops. Anywhere. Sometimes father
tried shaming her to rest, making light
of all her labors. Then for hours
she'd harangue him on mother-
hood and marriage, the stupid wastrel sea.

Only once, as I recall, did the sea's
stock rise in mother's eyes. The wild rhythm
of a nor'easter was raging and mother
eased into a kind of calm. Father
looked nervous all those cold dark hours,
the bruised sky suffused with greenish light

but she for hours watched the stormlight knotting,
breathing in its rhythms. I remember father saying
the sea, she's like a mother. I remember her laugh.

Aliens

The night the Martians landed
in Grovers Mills, New Jersey
fear took my father east
all the way to Montauk Point.
Like automatic pilot,
cruise control at ninety –
except his car didn't even
have a Philco on the dash.

I've heard the tale so often
it almost feels like mine.
Careening from doomed Brooklyn
in a black coupe locked like sleep,
past dreams of withered farms,
shingled fishing towns,
scrub oak, sand and pines...
a silent ride, thought frozen,
driven more than driving
till he came to land's end
and the sea slapped him awake.

And there stood Montauk Light
swinging its white blades,
trying to slice the night
into manageable pieces.
And higher up, the stars,
a young man's map of romance,
the fate he'll someday master,
turned suddenly a pox,
each speck untold disaster.

Propped against a bearded rock,
huddled from the wind,
he lit a blue-tipped match,
a little SOS, a minute spark
at the edge of the known world,
and wondered, as men wonder,

as I have wondered too —
What the hell should I do now?
Where in hell do I go now?
Who will come and save me now?

But no one came, of course.
Except for guilt —
in a flash he saw his mother,
my aunts, then gawky kids,
the four of them crouched
in the back bedroom in Bay Ridge.
The airwell window breaking,
a green claw inching closer...
And all he could do
was hold his own damp skin.
All father could do
was hold his own damned skin.

★ ★ ★

It wasn't until dawn,
a rising salt-stained fog,
that hunger took over
and ripped him from that rock.
At a cafe in the village
over homefries and poached eggs,
the waitress informed him
the whole thing was a hoax,
just a Halloween prank.
And she laughed at him,
she laughed, laughed so hard
he thought her eyes
would drop into the plate.

It was 1938 —
in father's words,
the last good year for laughter.
I would not arrive
until a decade later.
But neither of us ever was
the same from that point on.

The Missing Years

When Jesus was eight, he had
a special box, a splintery old hod
used to collect treasures —
carapaces, vertebrae, pinfeathers,
skulls, incisors, wing bones,
pincers, beaks, toad stones —
bits of this and that
from Nazareth's back lot.

Mornings, Mary, washing her blue mantle,
would sigh to friends and grumble
about that son of hers, always
trudging home with whatnot, enough to raise
the dead. But the kid Jesus
was likable, oblivious
as the moon, so friends tried to assuage:
"Relax, it's just a stage."

Joseph, who labored long weeks
at the lathe trying to make ends meet,
couldn't fathom the boy either,
refusing to be a carpenter
and hauling home such stuff. But
Joseph had figured years before that
his son heard duststorms sing,
and so the man said nothing.

Week after week, Jesus' collection
grew beneath his cot — the shin
bones of lame camels, combs of fighting cocks..
boartusks, crowsfeet, cattails, locks
of stock, babybacks, kneeknobs, bearbellies, hair...
the most common and most rare;
each day, a new treasure,
each day, a thing of wonder.

"But it scares me," whispered Mary
one night after supper. "Why can't he
find pretty things like coral
or pink grail?" "Or maybe something useful
like a nail," poor Joseph railed.
And that night as Jesus lay upon his bed,
they decided for his sake
to sweep up the crap and bury it out back.

Next morning, when Jesus awoke,
light coming to light, he found the oak
box gone, all his treasure
gone. Heartquick, he asked Mary, "Mother,
where is God?" But Mary said
"Get dressed." Heartsick, he found
Joseph and again asked, "Where is God?"
But all Joseph did was nod.

And Jesus ran and ran, and wept
and ran and ran far into the desert,
eyes like bloody suns, limbs
already aching, heady with new hymns.
And there did Jesus stumble
in the dream dust of Man's rubble.
And there rested in His story –
the rest being history.

The Courier

for Jan Karski (1914-2000)
the Polish courier sent by the leaders of the Warsaw Ghetto
to inform the world of the Holocaust

I am carrying the sea
in my cupped hands.
Not drops of it, not liters,
the whole dark sloshing sea.
Claws pinch. Nettles sting.
Teeth rip at my palm lines.
It hurts to hold this much,
to be so small and human,
running, running,
as the bloody sun runs –
west – carrying the sea
in my cupped hands.
The faster my legs move,
the more I try to get there,
the more I fear I spill.
Rancid fish and wrackweed,
broken shell and coral,
mark my travel like a tideline.
Everywhere I've been
I have sown salt.
Everywhere now, the rich
green earth laid waste.
But I do not look behind,
not behind and not above,
where the white moon
nightly is devouring
the stars, first in nibbles,
then vast mouthfuls,
bloating like a leech,
whipping storms
as cruel as history
inside my pressed hands,

these poor dumb beasts,
my hands. How much they want
to toss it all away,
to empty it in trenches,
to wall it up for good.
How much I want to fold
myself in pine boughs,
to lie on high ground
humming, to be free
of this thing I've been
anointed with, so
horribly, to make it all
mad fancy, mere nightmare.
It is not. Straight ahead,
face forward, I must run,
run, as the bloody sun runs —
west — and bring the sea
for the whole wide world
to hold. The journey is
a minute. A millennium. Both.
But I do get there. I do.
I am ushered to a chamber
of telephones and chairs,
an ordinary room
of the twentieth century.
Three well-dressed men
walk in, mopping brows
with well-starched hand-
kerchiefs. I want to beg
forgiveness, to explain
I'm just the courier,
a small man, insignificant,
that the news is not
the messenger. But my words
are lost in wind. The three
stand stiffly, staring.
They smile. They nod.
And I... I let it go,

waves of salt and bone
flooding from my hands,
drowning all the ordinary
rooms of this century.
And the next. From the sea
floor I start rising through
a maelstrom black as ink,
past the dead eyes of the living,
the live eyes of the dead...
till I surface with my hands,
two smooth and separate shells,
knifed open like an oyster
which can never join again.

Safe Places

for Barbara Goodman

Corners, for example. Corners
Of kitchens, in particular.
Or closets, behind the line
Of overcoats and jackets
Wrapped in cleaner's plastic.
In bed, quilt up to the neck.
Better even – under. Wherever
Doors are locked, double-locked,
Bolted. Windows barred. Drapes
Drawn. Walls covered with cork.
All the mirrors shrouded
With starched white sheets.

The Rainmaker

He used to rely upon rumor
to find work, farmers and their wives
eager to enumerate the hardships
of others – up north,
the corn was small as carrots;
out west, wheat had burned.
Too often, though, such gossip
proved just a way of gloating
or simply defense of their own
stunted growth and he learned
like any rainmaker to count
only on the sky – swift white wisps
clawed and batted by cat winds,
the lunacy of blue, suns drunk
on themselves and burning
for still more. These signs
now show the way. And before
horizons sizzle, before brown
crumpled plants appear along
the roadside, even before the taste
of dust, he knows what lies ahead.

Perched on the cracked gray planks
of his old wagon, he swirls
into a town, looking every inch
like a man who could work weather –
face deviled with arroyos, saltflats,
ruts, straw hair scoured white.
Hesitant, slow, a crowd
starts moving towards him,
pushed by desperation beyond
bashfulness or doubt – until
at last their shuffling stops,
long thin fingers knot,
and huge eyes lock in stares.

Used to be he stuttered through
the speech, now he enters it
like sleep, describing his induction
into certain ancient rites,
his anointed role to serve
those cursed with drought.
Up goes a gleaming pitchfork,
thrust high above his head.
But no, my friends, he shouts,
this is not some common farm tool.
Behold the fabled *kaval*, conductor
of elements, wielder of winds.

If they'll just procure some
water, a cup or two of water,
water, something silver, a fistful
of dirt, he will loose its ancient
forces once again. Promises
of cumulus, white clouds clenching
into fists, and rain. Rain!
The ground to break forth
in wondrous abundance, unimaginable
lushness, seas of green... The moon,

only the moon, hears him
jingle away later, watches winds
gouge his face deeper
like the landscapes he seeks.
Back again on the cracked planks
of the wagon, he rides night
like a storm – hears the thumping
wheels as thunder, sees dust clouds
as mist, feels sweat down
the spine like a sudden spring
downpour. Above him, stars,
dreams which have been frozen.
Ahead, more of the same.
The rainmaker looks forward,
makes the lightning rip, moves on.

The Fairy Tale Fathers

Belly-centered, obsessed with soup
And boots, accustomed to rooms
In which they smell themselves,
They like the feel of fingers through
Night's whiskers, the sound
Of their tongues twitching.

Every morning hums, stitching
Up a pant leg, planting white
Beans, grinding winter wheat
To flour. They wring chicken necks
With laughter, hoist gunny sacks
With ham-arms, love to make spit rain.

Whenever stars or weather
Define their world as tragic
Complaints become their prayers.
They bungle sometimes into magic,
Discover what is precious; this
They stash beneath the mattress.

Every moment they are breathing
They are scared for their own skins,
Puff up often into trouble,
Try to wish away their rivals,
Loot the dreams of neighbors,
Tipple frowns to grins.

Hard bargainers, easy losers,
Broke or flush, paltry providers,
Quick to chuckle at a small
Cheat with a peddler, seal
Deals with crossed fingers,
Call the left hand sinner

While sainting the stained right,
They grow fat from years of fright
But stay stingy all their days
With the beggars in their doorways —
Even those like us that
They begat.

Epic

Twenty years it's taken him to take office work again.
Bathed in white fluorescence, he sits at his desk
in a cubicle among cubicles on the 39th floor of America.
Here where the suitors wear pin-striped navy suits
and know from Pitney-Bowes, he watches an ambulance
flinging its red lights, off in a flash
to some urgent actuality – but he hears no sirens
from this height, only the turning of paper, turning
and turning of paper, like weak waves in a shallow bay.
His memory is like that too. Shallow now. And weak.
Wild tides and women and unaccountable hours seem part
of someone else's life in some other, greater epoch.
A sea of papers lies before him as he hoists
his Number Two pencil, rounds off a few decimals,
begins to chart the vast shoreline of morning –
while Penelope, assuming her position
in the receptionist's booth, unfolds the fabric of the day
and begins unraveling the minutes, one by one.

Istanbul

Here the place he lies and sulks
as the sultan lied and sulked,
lain low and unlaid, in the declining
years of his empire. Turbaned
now in terrycloth and ice, he thinks
of slippered boys, sweet and strong
as taffy, pulling the black curtains,
ushering the sun; still, he does not
rise one inch. Quilted in guilt,
Regrets Only morning-after, pasha
mumbles postcards, pernod and pearls
though he's so strung-out this morning
he can't even stand to pee, slumps
further into pillows, frowns back
to the wall, certain he'll abandon
plans for war games and a brunch.
Then the day leaps up and licks him.
The bacon in him sizzles. Something
like courage grouts the bleeding heart.
In a wink, he's off and thrashing,
halfway across the Bosporus, each
stroke harder in the swirling cold.

Postcards from Silence

Long diseased with silence, our mouths
manage an incomplete recovery.
Words form, but mine come out
backwards, a tangle of kc's and ht's
only transformed by using your face
as a mirror. You, though, omit words,
violate syntax. Before you declared:
I feeling am   My   is hurt the."
To fill in the holes, I must pantomime
hunger, spleen and abnegation.
That is what I do, disappearing
under blankets, you raised up in wonder,
writhing like a wounded bird:
"Colder me than cube ice?"

Of course there is a relapse.
Doctors are approached. An historian
informs us the problem is with the culture.
He summons a panel of mystics,
longshoremen, Manichaeans and paupers
to face the erring nation. America,
we find, is no more eloquent
than either you or I. It just repeats
its name, a voice stuck in a barrel,
an echo back from steely hills:
"America merica meri…"

"Deal big!" you reply,
and for once I must agree,
upholding what is sacred is the story
of our lives. But I still can't recall
if I was raised in Maine with a collie
named Zeke or in New York with a nanny.
Our stories have been merging
these long eleven years and both of us

fear the coming rainy season. Our phobia
is mudslides, the elements fusing
a movable grave, a sludge
which will sweep us down into the sea.
"Long too," you admit, departing for
home, teetering the rim of our bluff.
But by now I've had enough.

Thus I am writing you postcards
of places I will visit
someday. The oldest Baptist church
in SE Oklahoma, where hymns are sung
louder than the wind. Purple-rose
Las Vegas, where tumblers whir
and silver clinks into my prayerful hands.
Downtown Central City where I hawk
books door to door, pretending
I work to support you.

"Dearest," I begin on the first
of glossy photos. "Smoke rolls
like tumbleweed on the road I am taking
away from you. You think I cannot
travel, wrapped in a blue robe,
secure in wool-lined slippers
but oh how wrong you are. Even now
I am edging east from the coast,
reading my steps left to right
like print. On the stretch just ahead
sand has been spread, smooth
as pure bond paper, to record
the progress of my leaving.
Alone? Of course I'm lonely.
But with a little rain, city folks
will drive to see the desert blush.
When they come I'll sell my postcards,
the stock already printed with this
longstanding message: WIHS HERE OYU WERE."

Saint Elvis

He works in the back flipping burgers,
large and alive, free of tight lamé.
And when, on the half hour
he whisks off his paper cap
walks to the dumpster with the trash
the wind plays with his locks,
lovingly, soothingly, wind plays
with his locks. He's never been this
happy. Millions of burgers to make.
A million shakes and fries.
The crowds come now and eat –
they who once plucked graying hair,
tried to touch his swivel hips,
scissored swatches off his sleeve,
they come and partake of the burgers
of Elvis. Until moments before
sunrise, doors bolted, neon dark,
only one old woman sits, reading
her napkin, sipping pale tea,
lamenting the life of a tsarevna.
Elvis saunters towards her,
smiles like he's sixteen. "Kumbaya,"
he drawls and she does and they
dance slow widening spirals
the same way all myths dance
when the song is "Love Me Tender"
crooned quietly and low amid
the styrofoam and sizzle of our lives.

The Oyster
from M.F.K. Fisher

Conceived far away from mother
by milt set loose in temperate tides
the oyster starts off free.
Two weeks and two weeks only
he savors the devilmaycare days
of the spat, riding currents
wherever they lead
volcanic rock and wrackweed,
coral bed and sandbar,
whisking past lean fishes,
the unsung hero of his molluscan life.

Lacking grand plans or wishes
he knows only adolescent wonder,
watching himself alter
growing a new foot,
producing without willing
thick cementlike ooze.
For after the high jinx
of spatdom is done
he affixes said foot
to the first hard thing he grazes
and gets down to the business
of being an adult guzzling
saltwater, devouring peridea
and like his anonymous paterfamilias
spewing and spewing out sperm.

For a year he keeps this up
until bored by the confines
of flesh and brine machismo
maternal longings surface
and in the ancient way of oysters
he becomes a she. O now and again

perhaps to prove one can
she goes back to being he
but it's all spurt with few perks
and in the main
the mollusc remains female,

plump and alone in her oval home,
on the watch for boring nemeses –
starfish, snails, sponges,
Black Drums, leeches –
set any moment
to curl up like a question mark,
and pull the shell shut
on all absolutes about gender
or *idées fixes* on sex.

The Self-Made Man

in memory of my mother

> *An uneducated former barber, 49, living in poverty since he was horribly disfigured when he fell down a flight of stairs, has stupefied the Brazilian medical world by carrying out fifteen plastic surgery operations on himself.*
>   — Newsday 5/22/77

Children called me Werewolf,
said I entered Barra Mansa
every Friday midnight, ravenous
for flesh. It was true I traveled
rarely into town, but when I ran out
of salt or fruit to make preserves
I was forced to take the risk.
Old women, fat in black cotton,
crossed themselves whenever I passed.
Others threw stones. And I was quick
to learn to fear of bad dreams
walking. One night, I caught
an image of myself, dripping
raw meat from a cavernous mouth-hole,
letting blood saliva slide
down the eight horned bumps
which once had been my chin.
I heard me howling at the moon,
heard me begging her to hurl
herself on me, on Barra Mansa.

The moon, she would not listen
to the fever in my wolf-prayer
but rose with her old jokes
told in horrible white-face.
"How," she cracked and cackled,
"is ebb tide akin to a lonely
man's morning?" "At what time of day

will lovers take white-lightning?"
Spiders and ringtails laughed
in the trees, mocked me and sneered
till I lurched at the sky,
spit heavy on my tongue, and screeched
my name with curses. It was then –
precisely then – claws shredding
the low Southern Cross, I came to
clearly see the moon, a face squashed,
misshapen and pockmarked as my own.
Thus like the moon I could alter
what I showed, cut away my face
and rebuild what had been lost.

Authorities call me the self-made man,
a kind of modern miracle.
Over and again I have told them
how I started by shaving off chest hairs,
flaying strips of skin, slowly
reconstructing my left cheek and ear.
I have had to repeat how I melted
plastic whistles and shaped myself
a nose, how I fashioned a full-lipped
new mouth. The instruments I used
through the long months of labor
have been taken to the city
where they are currently displayed
at a medical museum. I remain
a poor man and hope the razor
or scissors will soon be returned
so I might ply my trade as barber.
Since the officials came from Rio,
every beard wants trimming
by the Barra Mansa Werewolf.

The doctors and the villagers
who tortured me a year ago come and
count my ears, marvel at my forehead,
ask me how I did what I simply
had to do. I answer, I was desperate.
I never tell them of the moon,
my sad disfigured lady, but she knows
what is true. Now when she is fullest
I aim my thoughts upward and
suggest how she might change –
tighten up her jowls, make her eyes
symmetrical. She does not listen,
the moon, she never listens,
and reappears the next month
in all her bright non-beauty.
I grow tired of my talking and lie down
outdoors beside her, that hideous head
gently rolling on my shoulders. Then
as sleep begins to take, I show the moon
my love, the way I show my scars.